WHILE I WAS WAITING FOR YOU

Complete Poems

1965-2000

JOEL WEISHAUS

Legacy Book Press LLC

Camanche, Iowa

ISBN: 979-8-9874823-0-8
Library of Congress Number: 1-12888658487

Books by Joel Weishaus

On The Mesa: An Anthology of Bolinas Writing (Editor)

Oxherding: A Reworking of the Zen Text (With Prints by Arthur Okamura)

Bits & Snatches: The Selected Poems of Sam Thomas (Editor)

Woods Shore Desert: The 1968 Journal of Thomas Merton (Introduction & Notes)

The Healing Spirit of Haiku (With David H. Rosen and Arthur Okamura)

Feels Like Home Again: Collected Poems

Reality Dreams: Diary of a Poet as Ghost

Jungian Arts-Based Research and "The Nuclear Enchantment of New Mexico" (With Susan Rowland)

To those Wonderous Beings who appeared,
and continue to appear, in these poems

And, as always,
for Susan

Contents

Some of these poems were first published in:

Trace, Rolling Stone, Illuminations, Monks Pond, Panjandrum, *On The Mesa,* Earth Times, East/West Journal, The Daily Californian, The Santa Fe Reporter, Jack Magazine, Wood Coin, Jacket-2, *The Ecopoetry Anthology,* UnderCurrents, Green Humanities.

Old yew, which graspest at the stones
That name the underlying dead,
Thy fibres net the dreamless head,
Thy roots are wrapped about the bones.

—Alfred Lord Tennyson

EAST TO WEST

Under the Rain in Brooklyn

Sudden rainfall in Brooklyn—
windows slamming,
wet tires hissing,
mothers calling the *meshugeheh* in—

the crazy ones who don't run
from under the rain in Brooklyn.

And Still They Keep Coming

On a corner
steeped in shadows
a few guys lean,
hands hanging into pockets, waiting for nothing special.

And it's not so much well damn it anyhow we was just
there doin' nothin' you know standing around doin'
nothin', when allavasudden sirens come tearing around
the corner...

so we run like hell up the street and into an alley,
        hiding in the shadows.
Then there's this screech of brakes and some bastard's
yelling, "They ran into the alley, Officer!"

Then we hear footsteps and so we're running again...

until in front of us is this high wall, and we hear,
        "STOP OR I'LL SHOOT!!"

Imagine getting killed for doin' nothin'!!

So I don't know what to do when Pal whispers,
        "If they catch us here we're bloody!"

O Charlie Chaplin
In Memory of Gilbert Stone

O Charlie Chaplin;
a harelip and
two soles flapping:

such cruel fate!

Met Her in Provincetown

Met her in Provincetown, Massachusetts,
saltwater taffy concession.

Hand-in-hand thousands of miles inland
today, can't remember her name or face.

Was I always only of her dreaming?

In the Dead of an Army Night

Day's heartbeat has stopped.
Cold creeps into its charred corpse
spread thin between clean white sheets.

The kid from nowhere unrehearsed
staggers in from his first drunk,
flings his only pair of glasses, eye
the length of our immaculate sty,
gags, curses, bolts for the sink.

They're all kids dying in deserted wombs,
crying scraphearted fragments of dreams
between my eyes
         I rise,
salute tall boots laced to attention,
strutting the long room, whispering
      "Resist…Resist…"

Dark, deep waxen eyes, the floor
looks up at me
        and sighs.

Boot Camp,
Ft. Dix, NJ

I Am Awoken to a Night as Walking

With the staggering light
the way becomes darker
                              rib by rib

mountains lose their tall collars,
adorning themselves with winter's cold moon.

I am awoken to a night as walking
                              out a high window

down I drop slave to the spot
waiting to receive this bag of bones
just as the snow receives my booted feet.

Shallow light splashes against a huddle
of sequestered tents, black trees, tracks leading through
frozen gullies, over soft bellies of fresh snow, past nests
of sleeping bramble...
            my legs spell out a slow
            monotonous circle.

A freezing wind grips my ears,
sliding whispers down
                        their gelid tunnels—
"What?"
"I think I saw something."

I look up...
and see the universe,
                  looking down.

Guard Duty,
Ft. Devens, MA

8

The Birth of Popeye

Black sheets washed in seas of bleached ice,
liquid flesh on leave in land-locked port,
bursting stars bleeding skies pale—

a pouted sail slips past parted lips
into a world of pure creation.

On a flattened belly of disembogued can,
a figure of Man as a child forever,
his mind stufft with spinach—

dappled face dancing on disprocketed feet,
as anchored eyes stand two-dimensional guard.

Forever Angel she will die

She is all the times that whisper love
while dying, she's dying, because

dying, the wind will halt in her hair
one day, a noose will find her neck
at home, or pills, or knife,

and a shadow will usher her through
one more night she knows.

Even the Dead Have Potential

Even the dead have potential tonight pinned
beneath diamondized klieg lights
            r e fr a ct i n g
crystalline streets shattered of substance,

she sleeps in the cellar of many a heart
and the heart of many a fella, manipulating
sticks of stone, till she flew home
an iridescent efflorescent big-time-box-office

star under klieg lights smiles spread on lips like
warm mayonnaise, banks raise rivers
of how can I ever thanks for the memory
of making me tonight by the light of the silvery
klieg lights.

                    Lights!

Summer Lightning Hastily Exposes Negatives
finding them still too black

Color travels in guarded tones;
shadows embrace, bear one another;
splendid nuances go unnoticed
lost within gleaming white spheres,

vast visions roll, blotted out by nascent wounds:
the dead have voted not to die into a gray squalor
where horses gallop the length of dreaming veins.

Only to a milky eye
does color vanish
into its forever bed.

Old Injin he was

Messed up on the Long Walk,
he caught in his belly a greedy bullet
and rode all the way to hell.

Now calves are skinny in the dust,
and the tent shows signs of wear.

On the horizon,
rain gathers in the corners
of his bloodshot eyes.

Marilyn

With her dark hair blond
        blinding a generation
        that buried its head in

               a saint because she died
               with her telephone ringing.

Miracles?

She stood full length in the mirror
        still believing
               in the flesh
        still believing
               in the America

that created her
in its wash & wear
underwear.

The Body

Face suddenly old,
almost without warning
renamed "the Body."

Head Nurse phones "the Home,"
and soon the Body is gone—

bed's remade,
fresh sheets ready.

Cancer Ward,
Green's Hospital
San Francisco.

Like a Child in Hand

Like a child in hand
umbrella flies off
taking me with it.

Friday the 13th

White-boxed ceiling and carpet
hide dirt and dull pain.

As glazed shapes stroll past a broken mirror,
the Beatles are singing in a crystal chandelier

above. On the lobby's wall:
CONVERSATIONS LIMITED TO FIVE MINUTES

and every five minutes the telephone rings to say,
"Give love a chance."

Words for David Meltzer

I search the eyes, the nose, the lips,
the words give you away.

I follow myself into Gautama's house.
Flowers cense the room,
while in the synagogue
the old men have bad breath.

The Jews have a word for everything;
the Buddha had no words worth repeating;
but you are still a man of words.

In the Mind Unborn sits Maitreya,
the Coming One, the one who will become
when not a single word is left unrealized.

I search the eyes, the nose, the lips,
the words give you away.

The Wooden Bridge

Ducklings float out of the rushes,
large white flowers peek from behind bushes.

Now in sunlight ducklings...

Now in sunlight ducklings
swim close to their mother,
tiny insects buzz the muddy shores.

Golden Gate Park, San Francisco

Northern California Amateur Hard Court Tennis Finals: Women's Singles

It is evident from the beginning
who is going to win.

But the other girl is tall and pretty,
wears lace underwear,

and cries after missing a few
easy ones.

Introductory Speech to Arrabal's "Automobile Graveyard"

Electric windows crank down
on a landscape of defeated metal robot insides
                                                ripped out
rusting under a hot reptilian moon,
shadowboxes powered by brainless wheels turning
                                        everywhere turning,
even children hear them turning while Master sleeps
silently spinning sardonic whispers...

                            Listen:

Cops in the heaven, badges rusty with dew,
call for all Threatening Things to be woven
into whips
            whipping themselves.

Judges, having given up
their robes hanging limp
in a closet it is night...

God's Eye Theater
San Francisco, 1967

Cats Scratch the Door

Cats scratch the door, old flea bites itch.

Cats stand guard middle of the night
meowing—cold moon, yellow eyes—.

"Pussies go to sleep! I'm up early in the morn
to clear my throat."

Cities bloom around trapped beasts,
cement pours into raw paw wounds,
hands and tails through the window—

"And stay out! Fur, fleas, piss, get a job.
I can't support you. Poets aren't pet food rich."

Cats too old for fight or fuck guard my door
middle of the night—cold moon yellow eyes—.

One thinks he's the Buddha,
the other's scared all the time.

Mountain Haiku

Peanut butter sandwich and a chunk of Monterey Jack
cheese in an old Army gas mask bag.
Marin sun filters through thin clouds and Dipsea Trail
begins its long climb through deep green forests,
bright Breughel pastures, "a huge pissing," (Snyder).

High above Pacific, cool sea breezes chill a lone hiker
disappearing around a bend in the road.
Turning, strolling back, boots tied together, flung over
a shoulder, short mountain hairs tickle feet.

Without missing a single cud chew,
cows watch a stranger inspecting an army of ants.

Old dung becomes petrified;
meadows become forests,
forests become meadows,
forests again, Muir Woods
mostly downhill now.

A clearing off the trail,
pine needle cushion to sit on—

> *wind through trees,*
> *one leaf*
> *spinning*

Mt. Tamalpais,
Marin Co., CA.

Three Raccoons

Three raccoons
walk through camp
just looking.

Mt. Tamalpais: 4 a.m.

Man is one bright moon
casting long shadows.

Walking he can walk
no further.

Clearing a small space
of stones,

Night, moon, man, one
bright meadow of stars.

Even On This

Even on this
exotic plant:
        flies.

July

Sprinklers in the park appear
from green nowhere,
drenching "Oh...

I *thought* I heard water!"
screams chubby young girl
getting suddenly wet,
two of them giggling.

Warm, stagnant air,
wooden bench on the path
to Rhododendron Dell.

Signs

1.

Bombed?
First thoughts as I looked straight ahead,
windows ablaze in City Hall,
janitor and his pail just entering, then back
to half-demolished California Brewing Company Building,
loose skin hanging plaster guts, bloodless,
an empty water tower scheduled to fall.

Crane supported by four white columns of fog, each
marked SAVE, hovers over the rubble...

Father finds me sitting behind a pillar writing
a poem about plush hotel lobby he's wandering through,
while Mother and Nephew sit staring at their reflections
in hotel lobby window, wherein they see me...

I'm two weeks later, looking at a newly-painted sign
across the street:

ADULT OPPORTUNITY CENTER

2.

The tower still stands. Through its wounded side
I see monumental billowing clouds signifying Heaven
in the middle of a furrowed landscape.

City Hall's rotunda is a golden egg riveted and rusting
in a smoggy Hell. Janitor and his pail are home
ruminating. No rain, no Black Sea trickling up, no sudden
blossoming, just a water hose connected to the broom
closet sink, and a sign hanging across the street:

EMPLOYMENT FOR GHETTO YOUTH

3.

Picked up a plump tight panted long brown-haired girl
on my way to Berkeley, listening past air rushing through
automobile side windows at how police clubs cracked
her skull on the steps of the "Halls of Learning."

You remember beads, I remember a young artist
explaining riots as an art form, a happening: rope
off and sell tickets to view, more for a helicopter ride,
more if you want to swoop down like General Vietnam
Zap-Zap and personally push napalm release button
for a crow's eye view of moist skin melting.

Any different from Nitsch stuffing calves' brains into
his fly? Or an iron ball smashing glass brick plaster
cement?
No different from sign buried in rubble across the street:

ADOLESCENT CREATIVE ENTERPRISES

Chinatown

1.

Hwui Shan beached just north of L.A.,
before 500. A.D.

Before 1850, overseas Chinese arrived
to send their earnings—as houseboys,
peddlers, fishermen, cooks, miners
working second-hand mines,
railroad builders tunneling through
High Sierras, wide bamboo hats
deflecting showers of rock
and avalanched snow—
to their families home in China.

Until jobs became scarce,
gold petered out.

Then riots, lynchings,
burning down buildings
of John Chinaman.

These ingenious energetic people
alienated, by the majority, segregated.

But cities flow even through ghettoes,
as when downtown roasted in 1906,
"that horror to the nose,
"that perfume to the eyes,"
Chinatown, fried.

2.

Can you identify anyone of these
photographs on display at Y.M.C.A.?

Moonfaced children, hair cut straight
across foreheads; women sewing
"the blind stitch"; men sprawled
on beds high on opium smoke.
Or long-braided queues swinging behind
families standing proud in manikin rows.

An old man knows,
pointing in tones of Cantonese.
His wife, 83,
could be helpful too.
I listen to chatter, feeling warm
family circle,
odors of chicken and fish floating
down alleys,
rinds of rotting teeth
in laughing lined faces,
gobs of tubercular spittle...

secret societies, tong warfare,
sweet incense and rare spices,
small cockroach infested apartments,
cacophony of firecracker/tailpipe explosions.

Buddhists, Daoists, Christians, Maoists...
how many millions billions Chinese it takes
to make a world!

Fisherman's Wharf

Orpheus off a small boat sinking
pots for Dungeness crab,
catch down from last year,
down the year before,

picking his way through fog
horns so strangely calm
on Fisherman's Wharf.

Rusty boat fittings singing
in high voices, miles of
pappous rope coiled upon itself,
tangled yellow seaweed,
salt-caked swollen eyes
clinging to slick black jetsam.

A museum of witchcraft and magic.
A museum of restored masted boats.
A museum of wax bodies.

Browsing through art and arcades,
nibbling crab from cups,
fingering picture postcards of Greta Garbo
staring into a faceless bay.

One day he could not walk
or sit, or stand to see
everyone fishing in twos
but he, he left,
not looking back.

Yet here he is again,
on Fisherman's Wharf.

Telegraph Hill

Where Mrs. Coit's tower approaches the round,
cold steel rings kiss eyes viewing the city
and mountains beyond…
until a coin drops,

lenses fog over and through
groves of blue gum eucalyptus trees.

After the rain had passed,
flesh air spiced with coffee bean aromas
climbed sandstone strata washed down
from Sierra Nevada; risen again
sandwiched in shale dug for seawalls, pavement,
ballast for ships who sailed home empty of cargo,
filled with Telegraph Hill.

White marguerites, christmas berries, red brick
and wooden stairways, streets recalled from
late night parties in apartments long forgotten
with people long forgotten.

Irish, Spanish, Germans, Chinese,
artists left for cheaper digs, by the end
of World War II, Italians won the hill.

Dreamed of an old Italian man after his wife died
moved into a one room shack
at the foot of Telegraph Hill.

"This place good a-nough," he said.
"And money? Do you have enough
to live on?"
"Not much,

but I can-a die here."
Stale bread, goat cheese,
a good claret wine.

After the rain passed,
I climbed the hill's east slope,
so steep that when fires raged

and water couldn't be hauled up,
homes were saved by pouring vinegar and wine.

These dwellings,
beautiful they are,
and where they are.

Grace Cathedral

Hobert went to Europe for inspiration;
came home with a hybrid of Chartres, Amiens, Norte Dame,
with doors cast in Italy, replicas of Ghiberti's...

Altars, pulpits, vestries, sacristies, trappings collected
from centuries of fished-out psyches.

Dig, dug aggregate from Marysville,
or quarried in Milpitas for arches, buttresses, pediments,
posts...carved from mountains of cold gray air.

Zoo

Rocks worn smooth from shoulders
of bears pacing in pit traps,
in Upper Paleolithic.

In Mesopotamia,
seven miles from Nippur,
was the first official zoo.

Marco Polo saw one at Kambaluk,
which was private, like the Pharaoh's.

Aristotle owned an experimental zoo.
Good Prince Eugene had a lion
romping through his palace,
"extremely well-behaved."

Montezuma kept jaguars behind jade doors,
and a buffalo, whose appearance in Mexico
remains unsolved.

Attendants and animals died side-by-side
as Russians herded Germans at the end
of World War II, in the bison enclosure
in the Berlin Zoo.

Chain link fences by the ocean.
Mangled shadows of Monterey Pine.
Powder dry camel droppings and sour urine mix
as peacocks strut, and pigeons fly in and

out of cages.

National Cemetery

Peter Munich, born
in Holland, arrived
in New World, joined
the U.S. Army.

Big, good-natured Peter,
his thick lowlander neck pieced
by Apache arrow, in Guadalupe,
in 1885, Peter Munich died.

Every year the nomads,
to honor the Mystery,
returned; finally settling down,
building towns, cities,
civilizations; traveling
to moon and planets beyond.

But to the Mystery
they always returned.

Twenty-five acres of khaki and blue
uniforms draped over hollow gray bones,
buttons and medals in damp darkness
shining where only slow-breathing
worms can be heard.

Can you hear them?

No ribbons, no ranks,
no advance or retreat;
no flags at half-mast,
no halting drumbeats.

New-moaned grass mixed with faint
acidulous smog;
rows of headstones sinking beneath
tall eucalyptus guards.

Eucalyptus

"Down south to tall forests (Kari-Jarrah-
all Eucalyptus) of Pemberton…"

Australia. To California they brought
the wrong species for hardwood harvests,

though Blue gum's good
for sucking-up fog.

Poem for Pets

Throwing his weight against door,
sticking a paw through mail slot,
getting disgusted, piss on it,
the cat wants in!

No! You don't belong here,
I don't know where.
Eat at human whim out of tin can,
what's the mechanics of?

Don't know? Better go
begging in the world
with one warm coat
and a plastic bowl.

Empty Bench

Empty bench—

rain
  sits
  down.

Japan and Home Again

International Dateline

Glacial ice and snow flow
smooth as winter lakes,
breaks of cold blue sea.

Nothing but white clouds
as seen from above,
sun dazzling still higher.

Balboa's ocean;
the same deep mysteries
that wet his feet.

Strong Shit Smell

Strong shit smell—
tails wagging up muddy paths,

cross cement dam,
plunge into woods,
walking a parallel path downstream
cross again,
balanced on a thin tree limb

scurry up embankment into bright
yellow harvest, husband and wife
working side by side hardly notice
a *gaijin* searching for his way home.

Dogs lose themselves in bushes,
racing across trail mad dashing into
opposite bushes...

Slow trot back to last night's sukiyaki.

Niiharu Village,
Gunma Prefecture

*Hilltop overlooking straight irrigation
ditches and fields—*

One large quixotic tree,
strips of white paper
fluttering in the wind.

Broken stone lantern,
sun and moon lighting
wood and stone shrines,

rice and bean offerings
to big-bellied buddhas.

Shiroishi 8 a.m.

Fire of dry kindling,
handful of charcoal
makes quick heat.

Drink a cup of hot tea
burning all the ways down.

Zip & snap heavy leather jacket;
walk out onto frozen sun...
and crack a layer of thin ice.

The World

Hibachi's white ash,
empty cup,
eight tatami room:

the world.

This Night's Visitor

This night's visitor from next door,
small figure squatting with *ohaji*
and noodles, warms tough brown hands
over fire, coaxes a smoking log into place.

We eat slowly,
searching into the flames
with no words but
each other's eyes.

Five Panels from the Monastery of the Pond Dragon

1.

A green buddha pitted
against two white faces,
sits quietly in the rain.

Darkness descends on wooden steps
commanded by a smooth-scalped
monk, "Leave shoes outside."

2.

Waiting with legs crossed
in huge tatamied room,
listening to bare feet padding
down cold porch floors...
flying robes glimpsed
                    then gone.

3.

Whipped green tea
looks like pea soup,
almost tasteless—

Bodhidharma's tired eyelids
served hot to Roshi and guests.

Roshi: When do you plan to leave Japan?
Guest: I have no plans.
Roshi: No schedule. Good.

Roshi excuses himself,
"Must catch afternoon train to Tokyo."

4.

Swept leaves all morning,
racing after each one with bamboo broom
sweeping the mind.

5.

Hakuin's footprints fresh in morning dew.
Hakuin's polished eyes mirroring who?
Who's asleep on zendo floor.
Who opens door, slips out to piss.
Who wonders: Are those falling stars flashing, or
police guns in Berkeley?

Rutaku-ji is located above Mishima City.
It's abbot was Nakagawa Soen, Roshi

"*Change Trains at Ofuna*"

Tiny towns hurry past
Ryutaku-ji miles behind

a peasant woman giggling
under her heavy bundles.

Where do I change trains?

Kita-Kamakura

A little up the line from Kamakura.

Cross to the other side,

climb the wide steps of Engakuji,
"A roofed gate with fine Chinese lines, but
without carvings."

30 yen to enter where
everything's fenced off.

Wandering through cameras
and cement mixers,
we reach the summit—

A little temple,
an old priest,
the famous bell.

Yasaka Shrine

Corman's in the Java, sipping coffee,
watching Olympics on the color TV.

Snyder's home packing for America
other side of town, Kyoto.

Upon Seeing a Victim
of the atomic bomb

I can't look,
without wanting to vomit
into the President's Face.

Every Morning

First thing heard,
"It's 7:15, Mr. Wiper!"

Born
Again

into the belly of a rusty tanker's whining
motors, whelping pumps,
paint buckling heat-blistered black coat
of soot-greasy fingerprints, dirty blond brooms
worn down to their chins.

The world is flat, a perfect circle,
a carcanet of dazzling red suns, strung
around the wrinkled neck of this old tub.

Maryland Trader,
Pacific Ocean.

Night at Sea

Night is loud
　　　whines,
　knocking steam
　　　　　pipes,
stars roll
　　　into porthole view...

then everything's black again.

A Sailor's Lament

The world around do drown.
Why doesn't the union care?

Can Feel Land Close

Last night, GREAT BLINDING LIGHT.

Thought spaceship, told:

Early Warning American patrol plane.

Why weren't the natives warned
before Columbus landed?

South of Portland

South of Portland,
listening to American Language spoken
in a moonlit Greyhound bus.

Feels Like Home Again

Rotting fruit in refrigerator,
cat smells and the smelly cats
themselves, back again,
waiting for flea bites,
piles of scribbled notes, books,
half-read magazines
from around the world scattered...

yet comfortable home feeling,
two weeks before leaving again.

California / New York / California

Four Portraits from Grosz

1. Father

Father looks away from
a flower,
a schoolhouse,
a churchyard,
a tree bending,
a plum sun.

2. Before Sunrise

She is a woman with hat on
strolling through the watery night
as if dressed, but naked to the wallet
half out of his pocket.

He is a gentleman with clothes on,
a cane and a porcine face.

3. Disrobing

She stands with her back toward him.
Tiny mother-of-pearl beads are running
around her neck in a nervous circle.

Hair pulled back into a tight bun,
satin bows hold her stocking up.

He sits in an overstuffed chair,
Suspenders slack at his sides.

4. Sex Murder on Ackerstrasse

Finished with her, he washes his hands.

The room's a confusion of alarm clocks,
half-empty bottles of whiskey, stockings,
underwear, lamps, and the sweet smell of
semen and blood.

But where is her pretty blond head?
(It must have rolled under the bed).

Fly Smiles

Fly smiles
as dog
snaps him up.

Lucky Cat

Lucky cat,
stretching in the sun,
knows where he itches.

Waking in a Field at Night

For how many years
this moon has lit
this walking shadow?

Earth Waits

Earth waits patiently
for raindrops
sitting on a branch
                to fall.

Leon the Lama

Night of December 13, I went to meet
Leon the Lama of the Left-Hand Path.

Must have written the wrong address:
found a schoolhouse,
windows deserted.

Gātā for Margot

Holiness is a snapping turtle,
"good vibes the devil himself."

Better to be Mad Bomber,
or old lady lusting after dogs,
than holy, with robes on,
counting your beads, holy.

Better to be Dr. Strangelove
than have one thought of
"I am She."

Filled with doubt, confusion,
paranoid to the deepest cell,
one works toward truth.

Holiness is not to be hooked
on, "Just one more cigarette."

On the Green Pond

On the green pond,
the sun floats
like sour milk.

Golden Gate Park

Sam Taylor Park

With eyes focused
on Poison Oak,
I sit on an army of ants.

Redwood

Redwood 200 ft. high;
a little green sprout
growing by its side.

Gesture

Rain falls,
pats me
on the
head.

Touching

Touching tree,
hand becomes

wood-flesh
flesh-tree...

Not being,
Nor becoming.

The Carpenter
(The Beatles in mind)

Heavy leather holster strapped to his side—

got the long nosed pliers,
got the offset wrench,
got the Phillips screwdriver,
got John Henry's hammer for drivin' in spikes,
got machine-gun stapler,
and the long tape measure slides back by itself.

Draws American wages,
pays American prices.

Wears Big Mac overalls,
gloves in the back pocket
hung over.

Works a drill with bit,
looking like a woodpecker
riddling through a tree.

At 2 p.m.

After five days of fog, a band plays a Strauss waltz,
a barrel-chested baritone sings "The Sound of Music,"
children tumble down embankments screaming,
young and old tan together under the afternoon sun.

No police in sight, no talk of war;
just ice cream, Cracker Jacks, Kool Aid—

A traditional American Sunday,
                                   only braless.

A Good Place to Work

Sunny afternoon—
Bees getting their noses sweet,
worms curling, gophers popping up
from the other side of the world.

One morning there appears an engineer
with plans to remove a few bushes, maybe
a tree, or two—build a road "in case of fire."

The next morning is raped by machines
perking sooty smoke over dewy red flowers,
yellow eyes twisted and tossed into piles.

Same smiles as those in 'Nam,
dead "gooks" slung over hoods
of U.S. Army jeeps.

Cloudy afternoon—
Dream of Tibetan solitudes,
                    a good place to work?
Probably wake up to reveille,
                    the goddamn Chinese Army.

Brooks Estate,
San Francisco

Three Death Valley Poems

1.

That stone—
try to look away.

2.

Windblown sand,
loose rocks, strata of
Panamint Mountains exposed,
rising around, all around.

3.

Standing eye to eye,
Coyote and I spoke.

Then I continued east,
where there are
dogs only.

Eight New York Poems

1.

a woman bejeweled with dog's
arf arf arf, little legs straining
to reach beyond her leash.

Flatbush Ave., Brooklyn

2.

Helen & Alfred reached the park,
knowing each other's failures,
carved their names into a bench.

Someone said: "Your names
are also carved in the Torah."

Prospect Park, Brooklyn

3.

A Hispanic man argues
with a pair of Jewish eyes.

Brooklyn Botanic Gardens

4.

Sweeping the EL's platform,
gnarled wrists twist toward
another empty dawn.

Coney Island, Brooklyn

5.

Hallway's pale bulb
lights a pale moon.

East 8th Street tenement, Manhattan

6.

Heard beneath an arched bridge:
"Where's your son-in-law?"
"How's that good-for-nothing doing?"

Central Park, Manhattan

7.

Washing her pastel pink density,
this woman would appreciate privacy.
Degas would blame New York.

Metropolitan Museum of Art, Manhattan

8.

Stoned eyes,
but so much love in his hand-
shake, hours later my hand's
still high.

Lower East Side, Manhattan

On Carmel Beach.

On Carmel Beach,
thoughts get tangled
in seaweed.

Carmel, CA.

Behind Her

Behind her thin blouse,
big breasts bounce—
a duck looks the other way.

Sign in Pacific Grove

MONARCH BUTTERFLIES
MAY NOT BE
MOLESTED

$500. FINE

They caught a longhaired kid
and beat him with innuendoes
until he confessed.

You Sing in Me

You sing in me
a sad sweet song.

Long boned,
blond-haired,
someday is
beautiful now.

What Sneaks Past

What sneaks past
as she strides by?

What's calmed, repressed,
laid to rest?

Should I reach out and say
"It's you!"

She'd look away,
while whispering "Stay"?

O Woman

O Woman,
shiny black hair braided behind back.

O Moon-faced gopi,
brown hips swaying beneath golden sari.

O Radha,
dancing on Krishna's big blue head.

Ten thousand years you've been
fucking me blue.

How Did I Know Her?

How did I know her
from the others
passing me in the street?

I knew her, she knew me,
as lovers join invisibly—

One glance tied the knot.

Never a Fraction Apart

Never a fraction apart are we,
yet each of us an entity.

It is as if we exchange ourselves
for ourselves—

she sings in me,
out spurts my song.

There is no life without her.

The Pact

The trees have a pact:
When I walk under a low-slung branch
they'll muss my hair.

Like a Chinese Sage

Pine needles, pond,
back against a tree—

watching the world drift by,
always moving I.

The Coffee House

Rain again this morning
wet umbrellas go marching by—

"If a guy walks in with short hair
and wearing a suit, would you think him square?"

Red & yellow hot slice of dripping pizza balanced
between thumb & forefinger, wedged into a
mouth swinging side
to side,
torn apart, ground into
a single swallow.

Violation on the parking meter outside.

Iacopi & Co.
Home of the Finest Meats
across the street.

Headline in the morning news:
MURDER SUSPECT CAPTURED IN WOODS

Poor Frankenstein.
Square cement boots,
Only wanted love.

Caffe Malvina,
San Francisco

In The Arbor

1.

Mary, is it
> Mary?

A weathered statue walking through roses
> & camellias
>> in the arbor,
> palms turned down,
blessing the empty lawn chairs,

rimless glasses, starched habit,
> a long of prayer.

Is she crazy?
Is the Order too harsh? Talking to a statue
laughing, imploring, little girl 80 years old.

2.

Is Mary
> Mary,
>> beyond the mind,
>> beyond the rising and falling
of the mind, beyond all the arts and deceptions?

> A plaster statue,
>> an old nun.

Dominican College,
San Rafael, CA.

Sam the Sufi

My country's full of patriarchs returned
from strange sect initiations to lecture
the young looking for Peace and Joy—

>	*Breathe in Peace...*
>	*Breathe out Peace...*
>	*Breathe in Joy...*
>	*Breathe out Joy...*

so sayeth Sam, hands fiddling behind his back.

Sam, you old bag of wind whirling in the dust,
gray Wandering Jew, come home,
curl up with mistress & rummy dog,
relax, let your baggy pants out a bit—

we're all members of the same esoteric sect.

Helen's Cat

She don't mess with things that bite,
got respect for human wild dog mind.

"Where these cats at?" she leaps,
      twists in air,
        runs down railing, back up stairs
      to sudden halt: Dog's there.

They both run down.

Trying to Forget

"For Beauty's nothing / but the beginning of Terror we're still just able to bear." R.M. Rilke, *Duino Elegies.*

Just as you think it's dead,
some thing like an animal
suddenly runs in circles

clutching trophies of gut beyond
consciousness of pain (yet pain
so terribly borne)
                              until dropped.

          drags on a little further.

Trying to forget;
yet flashing on her
without thought,
no reason.

First Autumn Rain

lustration to the shrine,
  that Being Earth

  Cold bench wet bending
          bushes huddled
  swaying in wind leaves
          spinning in wind
  rain stuttering wind
    bells hands
    wet hair wet
    eyes wet lips
          wet

RAIN RAIN ALL GLORY TO RAIN God-
        King
        reining Golden One robed
        in red sun
    burning through black clouds crying
        O Earth
beneath your warm-colored blanket
        O Earth
beneath your warm-colored blanket
        O Earth
beneath your warm-colored blanket
        O Earth
    naked
        O Earth
    naked
        O Earth
    naked
        O Earth earth
        O Earth earth
          O Earth

EARTH EARTH
EARTH
O
!
!
!

Arrived

From San Francisco, phoned a friend in New York
asked him how to get there—never did tell me,
just laughed three thousand miles cross country:

Fly 12 miles north from where you're at
on the back of a Blue Heron,
land in Bolinas Lagoon,

rift valley of the San Andreas Fault,
southern tip of Point Reyes peninsula,
Rialto Cove, Bolinas Lagoon now,
Dogtown, Jugtown, town of Bolinas
got Snarley's, Smiley's, Scrowley's,
got a beach running north; redwood forests
to the east
"helped build San Francisco,
                          several times."

Arrived in Bolinas at night, on the mesa,
a broad, flat land looking like Midwest
of the '30s overlooking the Pacific Ocean.
Roads are dirt, rutted, impossible to drive
during winter rain-season,
named mostly after trees:
                    Alder, Maple, Laurel, Pine…

Moved into a small house, a log fire to help
keep warm near the edge of the cliff,
a hard-headed windy spot, yet gentle:
yang-yin, male-female, forces join in Bolinas —

> *log burns   moon drifts*
> *out of reach thin*
> *cool smoke*

Steps

Facings take two coats
Harbor Grey paint,
steps three.

Soaking the dry raw wood,
earth also this autumn
needs twice a day soak.

Evening: dream of rain.
Morning: beaded steps.

Doss House,
#9 Brighton, Bolinas, CA

THE JAPANESE
GARDEN

Introduction

In San Rafael, CA, on 2½ acres of high-taxed land,
sits a 100-year-old redwood mansion. Here I lived
with eight other persons and an assortment of non-
human species.
Among the group was my old friend John Kielty Bell:
architect, engineer, artist, actor, and director.

Sitting in a director's chair, John drew plans for a
large Japanese Garden at the back of the house.

Bubbling voices rise on the morning griddle,
talking pipes and ditches,
talking rocks and ponds,
talking tea house *shoji*

a few miles east of Pacific waters
raising California's lean blond surfers and Kobe's
dark eyed children alike,

a garden took shape
first in the mind,
then as a plan,
then the shape of the land changed.

Stream was diverted, steep ditches dug,
roots suddenly bare…

at this point only the dreamer sees clear.

Spring / Summer

Clearing the Ground

Clearing the ground, frantically working the gears
grabbing handles, pulling levers, billows of dust...

O MAN, dragged over the land behind a machine!

Cracking freeways, libraries, universities...
whole worlds of consciousness
plowed back to seed.

Laying New Pipe

Where turds bob up with clogs
of toilet paper and Tampax,
mint trees and flowers thrive,
the line was cracked by roots.

One-hundred-year-old terra cotta pipe,
a young Bay tree broke her way through.

We lay ten-foot lengths of plastic tube,
glue the joints, cross the stream,
                    and on out...

The Bridge

The bridge was built over the stream,
so the Rolls Royce
        could cross over.

The bridge is bound by six pounds
        of nails
        whose heads cannot be seen.

The bridge flows on an angle
running off its sides while not
                        running at all.

Feeling for Stones

Feeling for stones hidden beneath the earth;
feeling for smooth shapes and feeling about
with fingertips sensing form, circumference,
and some thing holding it down.

Wu Tao-tzu painted on a palace wall
a glorious landscape, a mountain, forest,
clouds, birds, men, all things as in nature,
a veritable world-picture.

A stone's edge is finally felt, gripped,
and with one steady pull the earth frees
a different shape than thought.

Wu Tao-tzu opened a door he had painted
in the mountain's side, and disappeared.
Then the painting, too, faded away.

Rock Garden

Up a dirt road walking
  past human dwellings,
      round a bend in the road,
        a reddish, wrinkled plateau, its
       geologic genitals exposed,
          hauled away.

Tire tracks where the trucks turned;
  above, looking down, a round
    cold campfire; higher,
      a trail leads
        into the clouds.

This is where they came from,
  rocks of jasper
     and jasperoid;
dark red and light gray chert
  maneuvered with giant chopsticks, rolled,
    pushed, looked at from all angles
  before Western Sea is shoveled,
        shaped, raked
          by hand.

Sliding on loose stones where are we headed?
Rock Garden,
      "roots of the clouds"
              rooted.

Spreading It

With bell clanging between fence posts,
heavy truck backs into our backyard,
its pregnant belly turning over...

> flapjacks dropped,
> boots laced up fast!

In round-necked gown and turned-up shoes,
Omako supervised the work himself.
Proud son of the Soga Clan, he built
on the grounds of his mansion
the first pond garden.

The work goes well, or so it seems—
> drip sweat,
> huff puff,
> "Good enough."

Boots caked with concrete washed
under a tap, set out to dry with two
ponds drying in the afternoon sun.

Hacking It

Cast iron pipe sawed straight through,
blisters rising from hacksaw rushing
to meet the end, singing,

with you with you with you with you...

Scrounging for Stuff

Up and down America,
enough scrap to build it again—

we got 10ft railway beams,
we got 1x2s and 2x4s,
we got bricks and stones,
    nails and bones
you can use ten thousand ways.

You got a pickup truck,
    and an old red flag,
no need for storebought goods.

Lunch Poem

Slices of redwood sapwood:
a lethal lunchtime sandwich.

Laying More Pipe

With pick and shovel find the broken
cast iron pipe, pry out old lead,
knock off rusty joints.

20' of 4" 40-schedule ABS sawed
and coupled with rubber collars'
stainless steel braces,

joined to iron pipe where the stream
crosses joined to

terra cotta pipe under
tea house platform

joined to three lengths of pipe
cut three poems ago.

1 lb. brick dull lead melted
in a pan turns into silver liquid
poured into iron bell-collars.

Black cement's smeared over all
connections, a waterproof coating.

Taps turned on, toilets flushed…
give it all back.

Michiko no Takumi

Michiko no Takumi, a Korean with white blotches
on coarse brown face, arrived in Japan 612 C.E.

So blemished were his features, old women with
pruney skin looked like Edo Playgirls next to him.

So atrocious his appearance beggars would hide
their spinster daughters, and children wouldn't
bother to throw stones.

So revolting was his complexion, the emperor
considered having him deported, saying, "He
spoils the landscape."

*Michiko no Takumi, what madness could have
prompted your conception? What sadness with
a face the emperor scorns!*

But this barbarian did have a talent:
weeds became flowers at his command
stagnant water flowed clear; untamed fields
became gardens when he drew near.

As his reputation grew, his flaws seemed
to disappear. Until one day the emperor said:
"Michiko no Takumi, how he enhances
the landscape!"

Mosquitos

Mosquito wrigglers in the pond,
long black wiggling things
soon will be buzzing for blood.

Stocked the pond with goldfish,
Mosquito Fish, *gambusia,*
the fish all disappeared.

Is cat a bit fat? Dog? Raccoon?
Loch Ness Monster in our lagoon?

Touching It

Red tracks run up
underside of penis
and raggedy scrotum,
dotting belly, chest,
crisscrossing forehead—

Itching for martyrdom,
scratching makes it worse.

Where did I get this
Poison Oak?

What did I touch
that I shouldn't of?

Black Soy From Hong Kong, Preserved Shredded Mangos From Taipei

Wooden boxes from the narrow streets
of Chinatown, San Francisco, USA,
collected for tables, chairs, bookcases,
flowerpots, storage bins for firewood.

Yang Kuei-fei's hair was so black,
the moon, mistaking it for night,
drowned in its thick currents.

The Chinese People, who love the moon,
grieved so, Emperor Hsuen Tsung's long
imperial fingers dove into the fragrance
and fetched it back.

"At the dawn of Medieval Europe, China
had reached the noontide of her civilization.

"It was an age of great political power.
"Tributes were paid by India and Tonkin.
"The Caliphs of Medina sent precious stones,
horses and spice.
"From Greece, Emperor Theodosius dispatched
a diplomatic mission to the Court of Cathay."

Ono no Imoko walked the city of Loyang, 607 C.E.
His inscrutable eyes having studied its vermillion
pagodas and rock cascades, he returned to Japan
with the palace, grand street plan, and the garden.

Bridge light looks like a Chinese farmer,
head aglow from chanting,
LONG LIVE CHAIRMAN MAO,
before a breakfast of—

Black Soy from Hong Kong,
Preserved Shredded Mangos
from Taipei.

Sono Tsukuru Kami

God of Garden-making.

Is he from earth,
          or water born?

Of rock? In shadow
          or sun?

Bamboo

Slim green tough-rooted clumps
blossom amid dead yellow stumps.

For homes, fences, booby traps,
blow guns, stretchers, so many
uses and makes a fine flute too.

Sung Chung-wen used red in painting bamboo,
Ch'eng T'ang used purple, Chieh Ch'u-Chung
painted bamboo in the snow.

This information cannot be found in books.

Before Crossing

We set out to climb the mountain,
as others had done before us, in fiction.
I, in work boots, tired quickly, the boots
weighing me down.

We continued to climb until walking up
marble steps in the heart of the mountain
to a huge circular room crowded with tourists.

We had reached the border, and would rest,
before crossing.

AUTUMN / WINTER

That Autumn

After Rikyū's son, Sho-an,
had swept the tea room's path
three times, his father said,
"Still not the Way..."

and shook the trees of some
golden leaves, that autumn.

Sen Rikyū (1522-1591) is revered for his
contributions to Japanese tea ceremony.

Gathering In

Clear, fresh winds last night
tugging at the trees—

Water danced on rooftops, raced
down drainpipes, drenching gravel
and bare earth.

Get out there and collect those tools,
and get that rocking chair off the porch!

Boots left at the door;
woolen socks drying
on hissing gas heater.

Walking On Waves

Last night,
the clocks turned back,
everyone's confused.

This morning,
walking on waves
of the rock garden,
a young man's looking for
the yellow car for sale.

"Don't walk there!"
"Why? What is it?"
"Water!"

Everyone's confused.

In the Rain

In the rain:
        old stand with mirror,
        plastic garbage pail,
        rocking chair rocking,
        platform below rock garden, its varnish just dried,

everything not covered
        and the covers themselves

in the mind:
        new flowers, pollen,
        girls with brightening eyes.

The Woodburning Stove

Stovepipe comes in three sections
fitting into each other then out
a hole in the wall...

then another turn to
and through the eaves.

For manuscripts, rejection slips,
newspapers, junk mail...
cheaper than a movie,
more creative than TV.

Smells of wood crackling,
shadows whirling
on walls and ceiling.

Wet Leaves

As trees become bare, thin grass
appears, damp earth blossoming
latent seeds, succulents snaking
their way downhill.

Raking and piling leaves until
they all look alike, and I wear
a green woolen watch cap.

The Tao

Rained last night while
dam continues to hold.

So the water flows over
the lowest point, where
Lao Tzu found the Tao.

Against the Grain

Tea house frame is sawed with the bridge
light for company; hands sweating as the
saw pushes pulls against the grain.

What is a tea house
but a shelter from rain?

Red Sun

A red sun dips behind trees,
powdery brown and black
compost blends it all,
summer and fall.

What's Out There?

What's out there, stripped of skin,
resurrected for the New Year?

White whale bones stranded.
Prehistoric bones standing again.
Children's bones from the Asian War.

Planks of wood,
        life-lines, cut
        and squared

Wild Garden

A family of trees living
amongst a family
          of rocks, as one
     wild
          garden.

In a Piece of Jade

Crags and cliffs, steep ravines,
trees wild and free.

Tiny gentlemen sitting in
huts, sipping scented tea.

Elegant women wrapped in
whorls of silk, long tapered
fingers, eyes soft as clouds.

Golden carp sliding down
slimy green stones; square,
flat steppingstone paths.

A tiny Buddha signaling
the all-clear mudra,
freshly fallen flowers
dying at his feet—

All in one piece of jade.

Barking At It

Dark blue,
pale white
garden in
moonlight.

Bent Nails

Wall of tearoom cut and nailed
into place, nails buried and filled.

On Guam, living in a cave,
Shoichi Yokoi, 56,
Imperial Japanese Army,
was found fishing.

"Has President Roosevelt died yet?"
he asked in gravid voice not used
twenty-eight years.

Told the war's been over a long time,
and asked what he will do now.
Shoichi said—

"Live on a mountain, meditate,
a long time."

Late afternoon—
lost in sawdust,
even bent nails
shine through.

Sliding

Flying past garden ponds and loess hills beyond, bank-
ing over rush-hour traffic strung-out below, rectangu-
lar shadow brushes past dark green buckthorned and
Digger-pined Sierra foothills, riding the wind on a thin
plywood back—the sliding tea house door.

Last Touches

Morning:
Last touches of walnut
stain rubbed into walls.

White *shoji* shrunk
by the midday sun.

Fallen Trees

Clearing the slash of last year's fallen trees,
possible hot stops left through winter rains
split with a small hand axe.
Handfuls of brush and trailing twigs
are carried, or dragged, to the big fireplace.

Burning east,
   500 years after Genghis Khan
                  struck west,
Cossack heirs of the Golden Hoard
crossed the Volga to Sibir, "The Gate."

Cheremis, Murdva, escaped into forests;
Samoyed and Reindeer People succumbed.
   Tomsk built near the Ob,
   Yakutsk on the Lena,
descending the Amur to the Chinese frontier
they returned to build Irkutsk.

Mongolian Elm withstands "drought, flood, alkali,
insects, fungus, searing heat, and killing cold,"
screams of women raped, men's throats slit,
children's heads split,
   chieftains smothered to death
        the rest made slaves.

Terror was still visible in the rings of trees
when Russian trappers and fur traders isle-hopped
to Alaska and down within sight of North California,
where broken branches sizzle in the big fireplace,
boiling my blood as I stoke it up.

One Week Before Spring

Grass seeds, dichondra, ice plant cuttings,
acacia too young for yellow flowerheads,
newly hatched mosquitos, flies, and fleas.

Birds pecking seeds sensing something
trudging up the path, *Head for the trees!*

With small round but real stones accented
by plastic Mungho Pine and Pfitzer Juniper,
Mobil Oil landscapes its gas stations after
Enshu School, Kyoto.

On straight stiff spine, broom
leans against tea house wall.

Door opens, a bird flies in; bewildered,
banks & batters head against window.

A motorcycle shifts gears,
misses,
roaring in neutral—

The Old Masters agreed on nothing.

This Garden

Bay trees spread a dark canopy;
dead leaves falling since early July
pile up with no wind to blow them away.

"If the monks were here, they'd pick up..."
the greenness of this
late summer's dream,
always begun,
never to end.

Afterward

It had been thirty years since I'd lived there. The present owner met me with
suspicious eyes. I told him of my residency and asked if he would guide me
to where I'd hope to find the Japanese Garden.

Gone were the ponds, the rock garden, the tea house, the arched wooden
bridge, even the stream! All that remained was a feature-less field of grass.
Ten Centuries ago, Matsuo Bashō wrote:

> Summer grasses
> All that remains
> Of warrior's dreams

HERMITAGE POEMS

Introduction

Between the north and east slopes of Boggs Mountain,
in Lake County, CA, flows Big Canyon Creek, water raised for
city reservoirs east and south. I came to live for one year,
in a small cabin poised about 2/3rds up the mountain's side,
populated mainly by Oak and Pine.

> Planes fly over, the road's washed out.
> Fallen trees are bucked for firewood,
> or arrested by agents of the earth.
> This land governs itself.

> What is there to learn here?
> What is there to dream?
> Why this place?

"We live only in one place at one time," quipped Dr. Williams.
"But far from being bound by it, only through it do we realize
our freedom." To which Henry Thoreau would add: "You must
camp down beside it...and give yourself wholly to it. It must
stand for the whole world, symbolical of all things."

> Every leaf scanned,
> each stone peeped under.
> All pondered, all significant.

Several anthropologists, including S.A. Barret, and A.L. Kroeber,
did valuable work among the natives of "Clear Lake Country."
Jamie de Angulo, that irrepressible genius, collected myths, songs
and "old-time stories." County resident Henry K. Mauldin gathered
an archive of indigenous stories. To these scholars, and to Dr. and
Mrs. O.W. Hills, who invited me there to live, I am deeply indebted.

AUTUMN

Taking Stock

8X6 paces, high as my fingertips,
plywood inner walls, no insulation;
kitchen's on the right as you walk in.

Woodburning stove's in a corner,
there's a box for firewood too.

Dresser with six bowed drawers,
topped by old wine bottles splayed
with dried flowers.

On the white-painted worktable:
a ream of blank paper, and my
Royal typewriter.

There's a small night table with a mini
reading lamp, by a king-size bed.

A feminine-curved tree limb stands in a corner,
my warm woolen watch cap hangs on a nib.

Wooden packing crates from Hong Kong
and Taipei via San Francisco's Chinatown
are stacked as a bookcase five stories high.

Nailed, pinned, or taped to walls:
photo of Ginsberg/Yevteshenko/Ferlinghetti;
broadsides by Creeley and Snyder;
lines from a poem by Shinkichi Takahashi—

> *Late in the frosty night, alone,*
> *I cross an endless bridge.*

"Nude Girl with Red Flowers," by Picasso,
key to the fuse box hangs over her head.

A calendar based on the twelve moons,
informed by Black Elk; another based on
the solar year, re-formed by Gregory XIII.

With a map of the Lake Ranger Unit,
the whole world's under this thin roof.

Economy

A long walk over narrow ridges,
west, to the sea.

Fish and hunt otter and seal,
gather seaweed and salt.

Collect clam shells,
polished later with doeskin
to a fine sheen,

strung on the inner bark
of wild cotton, or milkweed,
wire after whitemen arrived.

Strings of cash,160 clams
to the dollar, slightly higher
in the East.

Konocti

When you see this mountain,
"No doubt she's sacred."

An hour after rain, dry:
no springs, no streams, yet moist.

A woman who had words
with her husband ran up

the mountain, and stumbled.
When they found her a snake

had found her first.
"Old Woman Mountain,"

a grove of Live Oak
looked on as they fished,

played, made love,
as they dreamed.

The People worshipped here;
but not at night.

On Stream-On Line

"If we could get permits, we would poke
holes all over Lake County."
                    —Union Oil Spokesman

Rounding bend after bend,
a low-browed behemoth,
its mouth capped, still
hissing, smelling bad.

Concrete shells, sulfurous cooling
towers fifty-nine feet high, pipes,
valves, magmatic steam, turbines,
hi-voltage overhead lines.

We open the heart and bleed the veins
that heat earth's entrails while the land
chokes under mud-waste, sky blooming
nauseating gases, twenty-six tons a day.

Picked up a woman and her child
who were are hitching into town,
                    "to poke around."

Bear Doctors

"One of the most concrete and persistent convictions of the Indians of a large part of California is the belief in the existence of persons of magic power able to turn themselves into grizzly bears. Such shamans are called 'bear doctors' by the English-speaking Indians and their American neighbors."—S. A. Barrett

Roaming these mountains, killing was their profession;
like berserkers mauling like a bear gone mad;
or a man in the skin of a bear; *Gawk burakal,*
"human bears."

1.

At the base of a cliff in scarce-traveled country,
find or dig a den, clearing a space outside for dancing;
all this carefully concealed with a steppingstone path
to hide footprints, human signs.

Shell & bead plastron six inches wide; a small basket
half-filled with water carried under each arm swashes
like the belly of a bear.

Wearing a grizzly's magic bear suit,
                              dancing to the right,
          dancing to the left,
singing to Sun-man, "I shall kill people,
you must give me luck!"

2.

Rambling the rugged Coastal Range
in the easy gait of a bear—

"When we hunt in pairs,
the one who spots the prey stands on a hill
facing the other way."

He's been on the road since dawn.
(What's that shadow up ahead?)

"Come!" The she-bear led the frightened young man
to a cave.
There she revealed her human form;
saying in a warm, grandmotherly voice,
                    "You will be a doctor, like me."

By the next afternoon, he was running, climbing,
eating like a bear. Four weeks later, she-bear's
grinning as the new bear doctor receives his degree.

3.

Walking today to Adam's Creek,
I'm alert not to slip and be treated by
the septic claws of a bear.

Hung Up

Nailed a five-foot sheet of plastic,
eaves to porch rails, stretched it
taut so firewood wouldn't get wet,
but the wind
                    leaps at it
from across the canyon,
shocked skin quivering its length.

Some nights I'm awakened
by its stubborn insistence
to remain hung up.

Through My Childhood

Moss-robed, misty Appalachian forests,
Henry Fonda ran through my childhood,
bald Huron warriors nipping at his heels.

Scooped water from a creek,
disappeared over the horizon...
never was seen again.

My Friend

One rainy day at lunchtime,
a tiny grasshopper appeared
at my table, a good-natured,
respectable, quiet friend,

hops out of sight
when I'm working,
returns when I'm through.

Doesn't lap my face,
demand to be walked,
ball other 'hoppers in public,
bite little kids,

eats next to nothing,
no turds left behind.

Useless

In a dream, the sacred oak spoke:

> *Being useless is useful to me.*
> *If I had been useful, I'd also*
> *be dead. Eh, carpenter?*

Shih's apprentice listened, then asked:
"Desiring to be useless,
                    why serve as a shrine?"

The master replied: "He's pretending
to be sacred for those who don't know
he's useless."

—After Chuang Tzu

Trees

Mostly Bay trees out the door,
pungent scent of laurel-
       sweet fingers.

Apple, Walnut, Pear trees
in bright sunlight
       naked of fruit
         this time of year.

"A new tree annually
    envelopes the old."

Always different, not just in seasons,
with shards of moonlight flying
       between black boughs, wild-haired,
         twisting into weird shapes,
     bowlegged, knobby-kneed, asymmetric,
      trued to their own beauty.

Brushing Them Off

Lady Bugs, swarms of them,
hitch on my bib overalls—

"Where you heading?"
I brush them off.

And ardently painted butterflies,
where the creek straddles the road.

Museum Peace

Dark textured hues,
purples and blues,
high cheekbones.

solemn mouth, proud nose,
long coarse black hair and
obsidian eyes:

"Pomo Indian,"
hung on a wall.

Losing It

In the end we all lose our mind,
but it continues…

A full moon appears,
but it's not there.

Twirling my hat on a finger,
it strolls outside.

WINTER

What I Said

Ice collapses into coldly whirling water;
snow showers from trees,
                              or trickles down
to a muddy mottled brown,
I arrived in town.

"Got any blowtorches?"
"We're all out."
"A lot of busted pipes?"
"You said it."

Plumbing It

When exposed water pipe running downhill
froze and split overnight,
we threaded
      then carried
            new lengths uphill.

With hands and wrists grease-stained,
lips sealed by the wrench's strain,
we heated
      pounded
          frozen collars
                free.

Winter Branches

What is there
     that's not imagined
     that may be a tree?

Christmas Visitation

On Christmas Eve, Jack stopped by.
A grizzled man smelling like
a stale shroud, I offered him the
can of beer.

Drinking in long gulps, wiping his mouth
with the back of a hand mapped with wild
rivers of white veins, Jack told me of his
recent trip to Adam's.

"Ran into a fella at Adam's Creek,
where them weeds come a-poppin' through
the ce-ment, you know the place?
And when he sees me, he takes off like a dang
kangaroo!" Jack slapped his thighs and howled.

"They're afraid of ghosts up there,"
my dry reply.
Jack belched and blessed the beer.

Splitting Between Drops

After hours of rain, dark clouds
lordly huff off...

> *lace-up boots,*
> *zip-snap coat,*
> *hat on head,*
> *stride outside.*

Get axe, wedge, 8 lb. sledge,
plant chopping block in mud...

and it rains.

Three Winter Haiku

Frozen tears—
Creek rocks cry
When they get too cold.

Lion & deer
crisscross
in the snow.

Frozen washcloth
scrapes
skin clean.

Fetching the Mail

Poncho flapping like wings,
I vault over the creek…
flying toward clear skies,
into the sun…

but natural weight
and inclination
bring me down,
down into the mud.

Thus, once a day,
resplendent in wet earth,
I fetch the mail.

Mind of Flesh

Get your streams rivers oceans
mountains of you, rolling sunny
meadows of you,..

dancer, witch, sprite, wonderful
bitch of you,
                    out of here!

To Gun Me Down

Half-hidden behind a tree,
she spots me,
her walk cautions.

Close by, she cocks an eye.
"You live up the trail,
                  don't you?
Didn't rec'nize you.
Must be the hat."

I grin, then see,
the pearl-handled pistol
snuggled under her arm.

Deer sigh, squirrels shake
their small gray heads,
that my own kind think
to gun me down.

Body Count

Rat poison
must taste good,
to a rat.

This week I found four
stiff bodies in the attic,
tossed them into the blue,

and a fifth,
still smelling of life,
tossed too.

Moth / Spider / Bat

Moth

Stormy night—
a moth for company.

Spider

Slapped a tiny spider,
thought mosquito,
curled up and died.

Bat

Scratching outside a window;
a small bat squeezes through.

Open door, broom in hands,
tiny imp's resting on the sill.

Then leathery wings *flap-flap,*
swish-swat…out the door.

Snapping The Light On

Snapping light on—
something's there to...SCRATCH,
can't find if there's a...SCRATCH,
legs arms SCRATCH SCRATCH
all night SCRATCH SCRATCH

With The News

Flows of ice slide past
crags of broken cattails.

The sticks splay & say:
Spring is near,

Veins pulse with the news,
muscles settle and wait.

Old Prayers

These days there's more faith
Spring will return.

Here it's been winter a long long time.
So many mornings chopping firewood,
lighting stove, scraping mud off boots!

Then new leaves appear, like feathers
tickling the air; across the hemisphere
the keen noses of farmers *twitch*.

Maybe I'm just mistrustful
mumbling old prayers.

My Body

My body, ancient amulet, carries wounds,
celebrations, the character I became
when my eyes drifted behind themselves...

to where stones roll toward each other,
fish grab baited hooks
                and dance with them,
and a flowering tree dips to tickle a dead limb.

One Apple

All winter
One apple
Hung on.

Who Survived the Winter?

Grass spring up in a week,
the creek's gone to bed—

a grotesque body, burned & bloated carried
atop a closed coffin; a wooden stupa, maybe
a phallus, rides on its charred heart...

an empty slab, highly polished, carried behind,
six posts attached with rings and ropes through
them, all walked in slow, measured rhythm.

Who survived the winter? The living
                                  and the dead.

Spring/Summer

Five Spring Poems From Po Chu-i

1. Visiting Yuan Chen with Li and Yu

Dreamed of Ch'ang-an,
faces of old friends,
Li, Yu, and I wandering hand-in-hand

came to Place of Serenity,
at Yuan Chen's gate
we stopped and hitched our horses.

Sitting alone, Yuan Chen saw me,
smiled and pointed at flowers
in Western Court;
opened the wine, and said,
"We haven't changed."

Joy's fleeting, our meeting
had no time for hellos.

Awake, I wonder if they
are here.

2. Freeing the Birds

Sun over river,
waterbirds shrieking,
wild ducks, geese, gulls, herons,
are sporting in the sunbeams.

Once came a dealer in chickens
bought in a distant town—
waterbirds soaring,
chickens locked in a cage.

Fourteen chickens clucking,
stuffed in the same basket:
spurs cut, legs in pain, heads exhausted,
combs limp. Not dead but starved
and thirsty; no food since early morning,
the butcher's shop by noon.

The way of the Old Masters
includes fish and pigs too,
this I have always followed.
These chickens brought this to heart.
So I bought them, and turned them
loose in Buddha's Garden.

3. Baldness

Dawn to dusk, dusk to dawn,
hairs fell and fell,
I dreaded the end!

Now all gone, I don't care.

No more washing it, drying it,
no topknot weighing me down;
no messy cloth-wrappings
with dusty tasseled fringe.

From a silver jar a cold stream
trickles on my bald pate;
Like being baptized with
Buddha's Law, such cool joy!

Now I know why a priest,
seeking peace
shaves his head.

4. At the Temple

Crane on shore,
moon through door,

a charming site,
I stayed two nights.

Glad-found this quiet place;
no companions to drag me away.

Having sampled aloneness,
no more cronies for me!

5. Me

White beard, red face,
each moment's a hundred years long;

head's spinning
        everything's vague.

A hermit, sick and thin,
this crazy old drunkard
still walks and sings!

Pollen Pods

Pollen pods burst,
drifting up nostrils,
            tickling within.

Waited so long for these signs
of new life, cabin'd, cuddling stove,

one good sneeze should
                blow me outside!

Maybe a Flower Sneezes

Maybe a flower sneezes
a pinch of pollen
stirs a blade of grass

nudges another,
a whole field of wild grasses
waving wakes a dozing bush.

Cold chaparral shivers,
fanning fallen leaves,
live ones too,

stems and branches swaying,
I sneeze, yank
the window
            down.

Earth: A Basket

Glints of light splashing on brown
Narrow hips, brooks and creeks,
Swirls and giggles,
Girls in search of willow and sedge,
Flumes and frothy plumes
Reaped from clear-cut sky.

Earth a basket of molecular beads
Latticed, whorled, invaginated,
Leached horizons of soil,
Cold gray gelatin seas,
Worlds and anti-worlds
Unraveled and raveled again.

A Basket Given Is Kept for Life

Feathered baskets brought to the wedding
With good-time jokes and grins,
Wash your baby in a basket costing 80 beads:
He's kicking, you're soaked.
Baby's carried in a woven cradle,
Top-Knot charms keep Harm out.

Acorns carried in a basket,
"The baskets walked on their own."
Acorns pounded in a basket, scowee.
Dropping hot stones into water in a close-
Knit basket: water boils, food's quick-cooked.

Prayer baskets are woven with sun and song.
If a cloud wanders by, the work is destroyed.

Some Neighbors Used in Making Baskets

Long shoots of sourberry,
Straight stems of young dogwood,
Roots of Yellow Pine.

Roots of Red Willow,
Withes of White Willow,
Soft whitish long-leafed willow.

Woodwardia fern dyed red,
"By slowly passing through a mouth
Chewing the inner bark of alder."

Beargrass is bartered from Trinity River People,
Sawgrass narrow and long, seasoned two years.
Redbud bark is coiled to dry, gathered in the fall.
Red head and yellow throat of a woodpecker
Is caught in a basket (maybe).
Yellow oriole feathers, blue quail plume tufts,
Green of the Mallard duck, a meadowlark,
Yellow or white.

New Designs Dreamed as the Old Take Shape

Folding moistened fibers into
"butterfly," "lightning," "holes in a fish net,"
"deer neck," "turtle neck," "pine-tree'd hill,"
weaving a door for the spirits within

> *these my baskets,*
> *these my prayers.*

The Pomo Indians of Lake County are famous for their baskets.

Two Tall Men

Shortest jail in the country
was built by two tall men

who hauled & heaved stones,
then got stoned themselves.

Jail's first tenants,
they lifted the roof and ran.

Lower Lake, CA

From Where I Stand

Wind's reconnoitered,
starlight's computed...

we name and classify,
yet this remains *me.*

Three Insect Poems

Mosquito

If I don't get him
he'll get me!

Flea

A hair stirs on my leg,
but it's too late.

Tick

When I first feel him
he's halfway in my neck
and I'm cursing.

What I Can't Say

Howling beneath the moon,
Wolf says all that I can't say.

Back Again

Back again, up from cities,
their manicured dogs growling.

"How's the weather been here?
"Nice day today.
"How 'bout a beer?"

You can't help but like them;
hell, they mean so well.

Battle of Bloody Island

A field of grass sprinkled with larkspur and buttercup;
squares of sod turned for seed, ramshackle houses
by a rough dirt road, rusty machinery, no one in sight.

As a boy I played here with my baby sister, a shy,
inquisitive child, and what I speak to you of today
is the way she died.

At dawn, a runner arrived:
    "Two white men who had deserted forty of our people
    in enemy land have been killed. There will be trouble.
    Many white soldiers are heading up the mountain.

    "Do they have boats?
    "How can they carry boats over the mountain?
    "So we'll be safe on the island."

When we saw them gathering on the mainland, we waved
and shouted. They answered with small puffs of harmless white
smoke. We laughed and shouted louder.

Then earth split beneath my feet, people swam through the air,
I ran, heart punching my chest, eyes and ears sealed to the
screaming bleeding bodies...
Soldiers were swarming off boats! Pa! I spun around and raced
for the tall tules, wading in, hiding.

After what seemed a long time, I half-stood, peeking between
the reeds. A soldier was staggering toward me gripping a
long thin knife on which was skewed *my sister!*
Laughing, spittle dribbling from his lips, he tipped the blade,
her small body slid to the ground.

A sudden cry hurled from me ...

I am Pis'wis'na, the hawk.
I will always remember this day.

Battle of Bloody Island

One fourth mile west was Bloody Island,
now a hill surrounded by reclaimed land.
On this island, in 1850, U.S. soldiers
nearly annihilated all its inhabitants
for the murder of two white men.
Doubt exists of the Indians' guilt.

State Registered Landmark No. 427

Breathing Free

Underbrush is raked,
golden pine needles,
oak leaves, on hillsides

the makings for a wildfire,
fuel for the crowns of trees,
heaped and burned.

Now the land breathes free:
groves of wildflowers,
clumps of poison oak.

In the Kitchen

Small ants by the millions
on the counter;

large ants climb the walls,
silent, like ninja.

What do they want?
How'd they get in?

Curing it

Not a sacred grove,
not Apollo, Diana,
nothing a Druid would want;
just a dead oak log
sprawled in the mud.

Green oak is tan inside widthwise,
pinkish entrails all turn gray.
In spring, with a sharp chainsaw,
cut to the width of your stove.

If you want to cure gout:
pare fingernails, clip some hairs
from the patient's leg, bore a hole
in a healthy oak.
Stuff nails and hair inside,
plug with fresh cow dung.
No pain three months.

When cracks appear in new-bucked
wood set wedge, not in its heart,
it'll jump out, but near an edge,
it'll carry right through, brain
        bouncing as the sledge
             hits home.

Solid heat:
        split and stacked,
        cured in the sun.

Plans

Nine months and born to what?
Mosquitos and poison oak.

Stalking past summer to autumn,
answering letters:
    "What are your plans?
    "When will you visit?"
I trip on roots.

Pulled a skunk from the pond
by his stiff tail. Drowned
in the night, this afternoon.

On The Move

When summer came,
the People moved
to cooler locations,

swam the river, fished,
traded their beautiful Pomo baskets,
made a Big-Time,
met behind bushes and made it.

I, too, would leave;
but my rent's paid
'till the Fall.

NEW MEXICO

Climbing Above Santa Fe

Flexing head,
boots genuflect against rib cage
bound about ankles, knees rising,

suddenly dancing.
Planting circles
of tracks, someone's hailing:

"Arms here,
but no pack straps!"

Following visions
to nameless peaks,
following each other.

Yes

Halfway up we approached him
climbing with determined laughter:

shirt soaked, gasping from altitude,
cane dangling from thin white arm.

Reaching the summit, we collapsed
into breathless conversation.

Arriving later, the old man just said,
"Yes!"

Santa Fe Baldy

Voices heard from across a field:
That's what...is Santa Fe Baldy...
Shocked when...You're at its angle...
What's over there?

Just Trees

Sangre de Cristo Mountain's feet are dusty.
A scattering of junipers and grasshoppers
jump through each other's arms.

Empty beer cans spread rumors of Einstein's
magic entrance, into which whole worlds enter
and disappear, forever.

Here our narrow remains pass over
nettled flatlands, soaring branches,
fluted trees where summer fears
no ending.

Rowe Mesa,
Santa Fe National Forest

Prickly Pear

Earth has grown dull
from refusing to speak
to this prickly pear.

The Grateful Dead

THE silent buzzards scan a radio
blasting off-the-road, GRATEFUL
Americans, a sunbaked beautiful
customized couple driving with a
DEAD fish, sailing over the sand.

A Letter to Lukos

Lukos, Amigo;

Illusions, distractions, fantasy, clear simple possibilities,
memory's symbolic world gets fragmented results:
cobalt images, vermillion mirages, your brain, Amigo,
submitting to balance.

Away old mud-world's mental forms!
An error changed glazes in your furnace
into an unknown order.

It's about spirit. Your formula paints art into life!

>   Peace,
>   Joseph

The poem was made from a letter sent from a potter
in Canada to a potter in New Mexico, I found it
in Martin Buber's *Ten Rungs: Hasidic Sayings.*

Pecos Transformation

In an ancient kiva—
an archaeologist and his notes,
were found as one heap of dust.

Shadows in a Field

The shadows in a field
hide poems from a thief
stealing strange hours.

Wild Crab Apples
In Memory of D.H. Lawrence

Like wild crab apples
ripening on a tree,
be lovely to this.

Helene Wurlitzer Foundation,
Taos, NM.

A Heart for Rudy Jimenez

1.

Twenty-one days after conception,
the heart bends around the brain
like a horseshoe, then trots behind
the chest's ribs for protection.

"In dreams," Dr. Freud wrote,
"the image is of hollow boxes."

In baskets, on store counters in Santa Fe,
a collection was made for Rudy Jimenez,
"a young man who needs a new heart."

2.

In 1968, Capetown, South Africa,
a white dentist named Blaiberg was given
the heart of a "colored" machinist
named Haupt.

By the racist laws of that country,
the two men could not sit side by side,
but one heart could replace the other.

Atropine intravenously dried secretions,
Penothal put the patient to sleep.

Shimmied down the throat, a rubber
tube was connected to a Laughing
Gas machine.

A scalpel drew a long ensanguined line
across pale skin. Muscles were pulled
apart, the breastbone sawed through;
lungs bloated and collapsed, the sick
heart shivered as it sensed its fate.

In another room, Haupt was pronounced
dead; his heart cut out still pulsing, was
placed in a cold saline solution.

3.

Bernardino de Sahagun (1499-1590),
Franciscan friar and ethnographer,
witnessed this Aztec human sacrifice:

The victim was grabbed by the priests,
who threw him onto a stone block and,
holding him by feet, hands and head,
thrust a stone knife into his breast.
After drawing the knife out, the still beating
heart was torn out and offered up to the sun.

4.

Blaiberg's veins and arteries were clamped,
Haupt's heart was solemnly carried in
as the heart-lung machine sang softly into
the dark ruby cave. The Black man's dreams
were slowly revived, clamps removed,
and the

      heart   beat
      heart   beat
      heart beat
      heart beat
      heart beat
      heart beat

....

5.

For Rudy Jimenez, $3,000 was eventually collected.
He went to California where, instead of a new heart,
he was given drugs and a free ride home.

Bringing Up Dogs in three stages

1.

Ice Age transfigured watchful marrow
into kidnapped canine minds stalking
wild game.

2.

Mastiffs worshipped Colophonian bones,
whole armies were crucified and beaten
into low-phosphate burgers.

3.

Prowling muddy streets at night
for the scent of prey,
Northern Gray and Pale-footed Asian
wolves sniff the clear high desert air.

Taos, NM

Hermit Peak

Spruce and Aspen grow in New Mexico's
Blood of Christ Mountains, where a hermit
once led the wildlife in prayer.

Who every night read, *The Lives of the Saints,*
praying, healing, dreaming, walking through
Argentina, Paraguay, Chile, Brazil...

In Mexico, natives hauled food to
a white *brujo* whose bones were found
in New Mexico's Organ Mountains,
a lance buried in his side.

Las Vegas, NM

Letter to His Wife...and Her Reply

> Slowly through the day
>   it gathers light:
>   head, shoulders,
>   breast, belly, and thighs
>   right down to its feet...
> R. Sund. From, "Taos Mountain."

Dear Penny,

Strange years have guided me to this land
where, in the shadow of a sullen mountain,
I live as if walking on Achilles' heel,
having bled not as a god, but as a man.

As my flesh begins to sag,
this mountain lures me into its dreams,
where time is wed to an old divinity.

How are you, my faithful wife?

(Signed)
Ody

Dear Ody,

You remember Onassis?
Oily slime, he owns me,
your palace, your son too.

I fear the Gods.
Mountains are their cemetery.
Don't bother coming home.

   (Signed)
   Penelope

KU

Up a hill from Santa Fe,
a road winds around
a junk yard and a butte
of crimson light

where saltbush and
ringed spires rise
in your blue eyes.

KU Two

Ruins of a village on a mesa's road,
running north with designated winds
through Espanola's sprawling dump.

Feet in the desert finally top Ku's
small butte of crimson light.

Saltbush scooped out,
ringed spires, switchbacked hairs:

we make skeins of smiles
in your blue eyes,

A Black Hole

A black hole is a lie
that sucks into itself
the light of our once
bright future...

until all that remains
are a few brave poems
orbiting a void.

Mind Streamed

Mind steamed green,
pine needles sat,
as crawling black pebbles
were sprinkled over mind.

Sacrifice

Lips given to leaps
can't pretend a poet
won't sacrifice speech.

What Is Life

What is life
when death keeps returning?
The hub of a wheel,
its spokes blurred by
its own cruel speed.

Nun

Between forbidden glances she whispered:
Christ, my thighs' covenant with you is
bleeding its vows!

Coffeehouse Conversation

"Have you ever been..."
"On a date with her?"
"Rock climbing."

Barn

Cars hang corners past fields
and a gray weathered barn
ennobled by bales of hay.

Floors whistle beneath its mildewed smell
swept through slats, machinery rusting
behind big doors sealed, shut.

Cool Morning Wind

Cool morning wind—
hot air balloons
farting overhead.

Albuquerque Balloon Festival

A Feathered Head

A feathered head of Mayan stone.
What seems a mouth is the path
to sculpted words.

Albuquerque Museum

A Round

Sun rose before dawn, when dogs bark with the ruptured
throats of wolves.
Here we are finally ourselves, grotesqueries, beyond
belief.

"Now you know what happens when you die. You become a wolf."
(Siberian shaman)

I cannot write poems anymore! My heart was filled with
tears, not blood, knowing whose voice I had lost.

"It was the ancestors of Indians who wiped out twenty-six generations
of mega-fauna, the entire upper tier of the Pleistocene mega-fauna in
the New World, when they entered it, from mastodons to the giant
ground sloth...this is our nature...but our nature has other possibilities."
(Michael McClure)

I still dwelled in the taste of her mouth, the darkness
in which she candidly lived.

"Change in the valley requires recognition of history, an archeology
of the soul, a digging in the ruins, a recollecting..." (James Hillman)

In the vast space of autumn nights we rolled joints and made
love until, leaning over the edge of her shadow, I fell into the
depths of myself.

"Shadows are the depths of things. This depth, however, is not hidden
inside the thing. On the contrary it is a depth of radiation..."
(Robert Romanyshyn)

Cars whisper from the valley below; clouds hide a freshly
stanched wound.
Trees sense their flesh is also their sarcophagus.

"There is something necessary to be heard under the rocks / something moving my blood." (Loren Eiseley)

To a cairn by the side of the path I add one stone. Perhaps, I think, there is still a place whose god continues to speak.

"Entrances and exits are hedged with rituals and symbols, for these are the points of potential disasters. With each crossing over he gains power, as do all persons who travel to the edges of order." (Barbara Meyerhoff)

Old instincts push me to climb still higher, to where civilization traces its roots, from where there is no return.

"Memory is not only a kingdom, it is also a graveyard." (Elie Wiesel)

Refiguring the River

Over warm seas the air is heavy with endlessly delicate acts of
evaporation. The seas yield their essence, sometimes invisible,
sometimes shimmering in the calm light that precedes the sun's
upper heavens, carrying salt from the ocean's spindrift. Volcanic
eruptions and shooting stars wear themselves out against the
wind's volume of moisture and land's prevailing oases, wind-
borne mass reflecting Earth's changing temperatures, moving
huge currents, repeating their profile, new conditions arising as
mountains' corresponding shapes, suddenly visible, condense
motes into clouds appearing as immovable creations, while
embracing turbulence, filling pores, cracks, sockets, channeling
fantastic obstacles from the river's abandoned source.

1.

Stony and streaked with the Colorado River,
the days that pass for its source
are far behind.

To the northeast, Pole Mountain rises,
Bent- and Carson Peaks breach the horizon,
walled off by the Rio Grande, reaching up to
mountain passes inside the sky.

High enclosures and grassy depressions more
than ten miles across irregular margins of gray
talus slopes, spotted and broken white of
glaciers, an immense bowl of arctic alpine
muted green.

Dig deep through tough tundra and
grasses, squat by durable bushes,
voiding water, steeped in their burden of
densely compacted snow.

2.

Motives came to the river. The ruling deity
had withdrawn every event, natural or imaginary,
which would have been something real;
so they had reason to believe that the gods
of the place had cursed it with the loss of nature,
as everything has its abiding spirit, not only things
that grow, but also things that grow dangerous.

The people from cities had come through,
raising corn from the gods they had sown
from inanimate beings.

In any event, new settlers were patching the walls
of ancient pueblos.

3.

Those who see that cotton given to the sky
drifts as clouds, then returns as twin gods,
who steal from the walls of kivas, they are
the people who prepare white paint on their
foreheads, and lightning born in another
world, and even the air bows before their
sacred masks, their arrows decorated with
mischievous prayer feathers.

4.

There was a king, a dreamer with straight nose
edged like a rapier. He had a beard, clear eyes,
and his thighs were packed like luggage.

He wore court dress with gold lace,
ballooned-sleeved embroidered shirts,
body armor, and horseshit-stained boots

that folded down just below his knees.

Calling up the legendary origin of nature,
he saw a river flowing to its destiny,
even while taking its thousand tributaries
into consideration. He saw geography as
a euphemism for all the great forces
profound and complex.

5.

Blue winds rustle brown-skinned thighs;
a deep intensity of timeless years are lost
in the dense green of springtime willows.

Unknown, unnamed muddy feet, fast water
rushing around them, move into the current.

6.

While irrigation farming upstream runs through
narrow gorges, the river nevertheless descends
from a thriving population of mountain anglers
carving rainbows in black basalt on the high plains
of New Mexico, the quality and volume of the region
having been sculpted by antediluvian volcanoes.

7.

Twigs fill the river. Chilled eyes stare at the sky's
lights dripping water into water, finding no meaning
other than an intrinsic beauty that signifies nothing.

8.

From the morning sun, a wounded beast
closes its wings and drops down to a field

mouse scurrying through the sage
with great confidence in its own domain.

Central Avenue, Albuquerque

A street where traffic rubs against low
bramble and insolent boulders
growing and sitting between lanes.

Rushing eyes glimpse in opposite directions.
Marginal bushes thrive in pollution that defies
straight lines.

The meridian's traffic separates itself,
shaping time into barely moving lives.

For The Brothers

Moments grow bare in an ossuary fishing for people,
dusting history's jaundiced millions, exposing riven
flames, churning sparse regrets.

Known through saints drinking the world as a fish,
a rough road rises to the Eucharist's swales,
silently shrugging, whiffling aspirations from atop
the chapel's spiked peak, as the desert's silence
sings vespers.

The Charma River is smooth today. Mud off the main
road frames a round sky crossing these few men with
wildflowers chanting, "All's not dust left behind."

In memory of Thomas Merton, who visited the
Monastery of Christ in the Desert twice in 1968,
in search of a hermitage, the last year of his life.

As If a Lecture by Derrida

"I," the name, called to its lean expanse.

Advance by giving cryptic repetitions,

indecipherable legible gestures
in inconsolable unnamable moves,
in a voice disappointing itself.

At this moment, if the order is properly
followed, be a Fallen One knowing
an earth where days remain bottomless,
requiring our better moments.

Interlaced vowels work among accents
that are nearer, or perhaps ancient,
even monumental, or what promises
to give by decomposition, speaking
as a lapse, delaying where necessary,
making the mute indifferent.

Jealousy will be effaced here,
an "I" that accounts for itself.

Artaud

Antonin's impatient cigarette effaces his hands,
unfolding arrogant masks of enchanted gestures,
calling up spectacles among scarred masterpieces,
seeing his mind as an unfinished glyph.

Tumbling Still

Tumbling still coupled in
waiting in myself, holding
a lonely wing's outward space
still, a still pandemonium.

Miró Critique

Without pretension to liquid ether,
chance's mysterious signs are alive,
controlling a stage, an impression,
an atmosphere floating that conveys
rudimentary events.

Birth forms subtleties that envelop
a background beyond those compulsive
bodies that signify the world,
striking revelations, encountering an
unadulterated thing saying, "I'm in a
Bach mood."

And those that are simply vague,
incongruous, whose incompatible
colors, in their most gaseous and
cosmic distances, are imminently
prone to disaster.

Nämforsen

"In the late spring, the roar of the water can be heard from
a considerable distance. The tree-clad cliffs forming the northern
riverbanks rise here to a height of more than 60 meters providing
a panoramic view. In midst of an expanse of towering pine forest
the turbulent water crashes over the rocks and whirls in a series
of magnificent rapids, the last barrier before a long narrow inlet of
the open sea." -C. Tilley, *Material Culture and Text.* London, 1991.

Waters rise margins surrounding an expanse of northern
rivers pecked open, a fascinating series of long towering
whirls amidst cliffs, pines, and polished barriers.

By this flows the force of water's construction transfiguring
ice and vegetation into a mashup of turbulent surfaces,
of bare inlets, and glossy rapids, where salmon become
fishermen transformed by their catch.

Your Name, This Net
for Alan Sondheim

Traced against the empty, traced
through the header, it's a waste of
the essence, of the body of
canons.

Everywhere is artificial,
a waste of depth,
nothing works in depth.

Wrap, don't desire (Spinoza).
Quantum tunnels are ghosts
crossing over to the Other.

Outside my window, nothing is named.
I look through and know there
were lovers in those ashes,
traced in memories that hold the door open.

I cry over the threshold, "It's all empty!"
Dark angels fly past wrapped in bodies of glass.

Look for your name in the depth,
in the darkness, in the rapture
of nothingness.

A Poem Addressed to Robert Creeley on His Poem, "Histoire de Florida."

We begin with mirrors, ancient portals —
water, burnished wood, metal, any surface
that reflects "brother face," as to pass through,
beyond the world we commonly experience, or
think we do. A split here; another you facing you.

Today I am apposite to Florida, an inland shore,
yet tied to the sea by commerce and tradition,
drawn to that "simple ending," as you say;
and to so many "little deaths," as Patchen said,
in so much in pain, so *wronged.* Not like Nitsch,
whom you honor for the sake of art history,
chopped his penis like so much sushi. Not the
scientific method: who would repeat this
experiment to prove the artist mad?

Your anecdotes, Bob, are a vast community
providing missing links. We have the skulls of
who we were, and who we are; but who we might
become, given time, it seems are in the interstices.
No separation but in time.

Death is both signifier and signified. Does the sign
say STOP or GO (?) Your time was up too soon.
How many poems we now cherish would not have
been made! A poem appears from whose death?

With Leary, you say, he didn't "die." He passed like
one passes gas. (A clown, by trade, Tim would
have laughed.)

It is almost the next day. All I have to do is wait and
it happens.

The Hopi say they must perform rituals, or else the
sun won't rise. (It doesn't. We turn.)
It has to do with apparent flow. The crone eats from
a paper bag while the young are indefatigable
in their essence.

Why do we get old so fast?
What did we accomplish during those years?
Why must we accomplish anything?
There is nothing to wait for that isn't here.

The illusion of surplus, of storage. I feel,
so as not to fade, I must remain invisible.

Ever since the year before my father died,
I've arrived in Florida. Stevens was a voyeur
here. Frost's wife died upstairs, in Gainesville,
a university town, of course.

Kerouac died choking on a mug of sour Fame.
And your pathos, being a man, whose words
are as if carved in his cells by an "anonymous
hand," as in Mandelstam's poem, to which you
don't confess. I take history with a drop of brine
that stings the tongue.

But what is Florida without alligators?
I've got one; yours, too, is stored in a "book."
Books store the past more consistently than
the brain, which shrinks, Are we inside,
or outside? I'm alone, and still alive, while you
say: *No one's alone/No world's that small…*

Florida must have predators with sharp teeth.
Here's one that ate Ponce de Leon in one gulp.
(Ponce actually died from an ambiguous arrow.)

You're getting it right! And there is also the humility
of decay. Bodies become humus; souls are born
like drops of fresh dew. Not only is this world one,
if you can get there, the last one is also one.

I went to the beach to collect the ribs of things,
only to find cigarette butts and used condoms;
some shards of shells with nothing alive inside.

So Mother's almost blind; Sister's in Florida too.
Friends suddenly appear on my screen, writing
"What's happening?" "I just returned from Paris."
"Are we related?" *In Florida. Like nothing else.*

ADDENDUM

These are early experiments, written mainly during 1965 and published in *Trace,* a journal of experimental writing edited by James Boyer May.

A Sea Gull Gliding Gently

A sea gull gliding gently
Through an invisible harp
Became a Vision outstretched,
As a flame under glass.

Voices flickered before my eyes,
Painting dense shadows
On a resurrected ear:

Her hair blowing to her shoulders,
Kissing them,
Flooding her back
              with gold.

Just to be one long stand,
I would never fly away,
I would never fly away.

Lamps Are Darkened for The Last Time
her body

She gathers light before her,
daring dreams to
                Lips
   slip open
       silence sings—
In solstice nights above the sky,
even saints fall to sleep
                  but I

touch fractions
of perennial wonder,
woven thunder corked
by two taut nipples,
outlawed eyes
breaking into heaven's vaults,
looting with meticulous haste
all intangible in
defined space.

Canticles escape her heart,
bearing ghosts beyond
                thighs
   slide open
       motion clings…

Memory scores tjurunga laughter,
hereafter, there is less to die.

'Tis Better to Marry Than To Live With Wonder

glancing
    upward
it is bottom
les
s c(old
lights tossed up
by the e(yes of man
ceasing to question
begins to understand.

th
    us those long
thin
    shadows
settled over a full nest
& One
morning a frosty dawn
    beckons.

Sweet As Its Juice she was

I had this girl,
ripe as a plum,
sweet as its juice
she was.

It was just for me
she'd toss her head,
for me she'd open,
and lick my swollen thumb.

"Hellava nice night, Darlin',"
she'd like to mimic
a Tennessee Williams
blush of white trash.

Waiting for a bus one night,
both shivering a bit—
she took my hand,
I kissed her salty tears.

The Sophists

Sun Gold left its halo dissolving in the Western sky.
Last rays knifed through trees, setting them on fire.
As Night's blue slowly metamorphosized,
Venus lifted her angelic face and smiled.
Moon's silver shook loose a dusty cloud, drenching
the tranquil sophists in lemon phosphorescence...

They sat on a mountaintop in the valley of Geber.
They sat with nicotine-stained fingers.
They sat with teddy bear minds.

"The gist of it is that I'm tired of waiting for him
to appear.
"But he's already here, you know that.
"More than rumors?
"Strings around necks; men stretched to...
"Imagination!
"No! No!
"Then what?
"Fishes.
"Left-handed fishes?
"Yes, yes. Then you *do* know.
"Only rumors.
"Then hear more. Thousands freed from...
"Enough! Just tell me, why the pending
holocaust?
"He died.
"Oh? Pity. We could use him now.
"I wonder.

Leaving

Are the birds telling their story
of how frightened they were
the first time they flew,
two in the morning, raining?

About the Author

At age 19 Joel Weishaus a Jr. Executive at a Madison Avenue agency, specializing in movie advertising. He moved to San Francisco in 1964, and was a student in the University of California, Berkeley, Department of Oriental Languages, and Literary Editor of the student newspaper. During the 1980s, living in Albuquerque, New Mexico, he was a photography critic for *Artspace: A Quarterly of Contemporary Southwest Art,* Adjunct Curator at the University of New Mexico's Museum of Fine Arts, and a Writer-in-Residence at UNM's Center for Southwest Research. For several years he was Visiting Faculty in Portland State University's English Department and was a Visiting Scholar and Research Fellow at the University of California, Santa Barbara. His current research is sponsored by Portland State University's Philosophy Department. For the past ten years he has been the Artist-in-Residence at Pacifica Graduate Institute, Carpinteria, California.